Powerful Miracle Manifestation Book
by
Spiritual Teacher
Anna Simon

About the Author

Psychic Medium, Clairvoyant, Channeler, Energy Practitioner, and Spiritual Teacher.

Anna Simon has been an internationally known as a psychic medium, spiritual teacher, mentoring for nearly 20 years. She talks directly to your Angels and Guides. She is uncannily accurate with names, dates, details in her readings. She specializes in love and relationship. Her passion is teaching others how to reach their highest potential through her gifts of mentoring, mediumship, spiritual intuitive, psychic readings and high energy practitioner.

Born with the 'gift of sight', Anna also possesses the ability to connect to the 'other side' as a medium. As a little girl, she recognized that she had special abilities; however, she did not fully comprehend her gifts as a psychic medium. She was unaware that she was communicating with Angels. She would have visions and receive messages for others. As the years passed, she began to have encounters with psychic phenomena. During this time, as a young adult, she offered psychic readings for friends and family. This further propelled her gift and enabled her to hone her craft to become validated in her work today.

Anna is different from other psychics because through her teachings she gives her clients the tools to lead a better life. She will teach you how to manifest your true desires with simple and effective techniques. Anna empowers you by giving you accurate psychic readings including names, dates, and descriptions of your true soul mate and spiritual path. Her healings are done through loving Universal Energy. God has given her great gifts that she wants to share with you to help you to be happy in life.

Today, Anna is doing her life's work and true calling - attracting wonderful people into her life. She manifested a loving happy marriage, financial success and true inner peace. She wants you to be as happy and fulfilled as she is in her life.

So she has written this book in which is powerful course to help you obtain your true happiness today

Table of Contents

introduction:

Manifesting Book Course Teachings
by Spiritual Teacher Anna M Simon

Become full in your power.

This particular course is not taught on Anna's shows or in her Spiritual Blogs. This is a true powerful course, only meant for the people who are ready to move forward and be in their full power. Receive all, and be who you were meant to be."

Note: The content of this course was channeled through Anna by the Archangels Michael, Raphael, Gabriel and Uriel. The messages dictated by the Archangels are a true blessing and as such students are required to commit to their studies with open minds and emotions. It is of the utmost importance that the studies be conducted without interruption to the sequence of the daily lessons and that they fulfill their assignments on a timely basis. Structure within the course is set so as to give the student the most benefit and success for achieving Higher Vibration from within.
It is our wish that you recognize your true Self and find the Light worker within you. Blessings to you and may you be filled with love and light…

Manifestation Course Day 1

"This lesson begins with releasing the past. Yes, you must release all past experiences. Clear out the old and allow for the new. Let us begin by taking a few deep breaths.

I want you to clear your mind. As you clear your mind with each breath, release all negative issues from childhood and beyond. When I say release, I mean let go of all issues of abandonment that made you feel that you were alone and frightened. Release all of the pain. You need to clear these issues before you can come into your power, which will be coming to you soon.

As you release and give all negative aspects to the universe, ask for the positive love and light to come through you. Feel the energy of the loving universe.

Also, visualize your new life beginning as we speak. Look for today not tomorrow. Live in the present and as you live in the present you are shaping your future. Allow the loving light to heal old wounds.

You are being cleansed and the healing begins from the top of your head to the end of your feet. Feel the loving energy come through you. Allow yourself to be free from any past bounds.

Say this Affirmation in the morning:

"I am the child of a loving God and I dare to prosper now."

"Say it three times in succession. Say it with faith and conviction
Sometime today, get some clearing done.
Whether it is your desk at work or your closet at home start clearing out the old to allow for the new.
Do not try to remember past lessons. The seeds have already been planted in your subconscious. Allow the healing to begin. Your cells are changing and as we speak you are being reborn into your new powerful self."

For nighttime take a nice shower or bath. If you desire, soak in lavender. Sea salt is also highly recommended. If you bought my spiritual mist, spray yourself twice in the day and twice at night for true alignment.

After you've completed the first lesson, email me within twenty- four hours to tell me how you feel.

Manifestation Course Day 2

"Good morning and welcome to the loving changes in your life. At this time you have already made it through the first day of the course. Your mind might already be fighting the changes. When your mind starts to fight the changes release it to your Angels and Guides. Once it is released, you will sense the change and begin to feel the peace.

This course is no only about manifesting, it is also about becoming, One with the Universe. Loving yourself is important to connecting to the Oneness of the universe.

Start today by giving thanks for your new and loving self. The first step to manifesting and connecting to the universe is to love yourself and forgive yourself, as well as forgiving others for past issues. Forgiving is another step necessary in order to achieve higher consciousness.

You are a child of a loving GOD and to be one with the Universe is to forgive. Have compassion and understanding. Aren't you one with every living being on this earth?"

Close your eyes and look within. Ask your Angels what it is that you need to clear out of your life in order to start manifesting all that you desire.

They will answer you, but don't expect them to talk out loud. They will give you answers through other people, dreams and thoughts.

Let's end the day with "Ask and you shall receive." Start by asking the Angels to help you on your mission. They will begin helping you and it will be obvious when it comes.

Write in your journal tonight and send love and thanks to someone who has helped you in your past.

You will see that the healing will begin and you will start aligning with the Universe. You will begin to manifest what you desire.

You are reading this because you want to make a difference and making a difference is a lot of responsibility. You will become stronger and more confident as this course goes on.

Give thanks tonight and ask your angels to manifest something for you. Choose something small, something that will make you understand that you are aligned with the loving Universe.

Affirmations for the Day

"I love my Self and forgive my Self for all past actions."

"I am now coming into my power and I dare to see results now."

Say this in the morning and evening in three successions. And find some peaceful mediation or relaxing smoothing bath to relax you. Once you do that relax and go to bed. As you fall asleep you will feel the relaxation and peace within.

Manifestation Course Day 3

Today's Course is about reflection. We need to go back these past two days and reflect on what you have noticed. Are you beginning to notice a change? Have you followed the course exactly how it was written or have you put your own twist to it? If you followed the course exactly how it was written then you should see results quickly. If you have not followed the course exactly, results will be different and you may need to repeat steps one and two. Please call or email if you have any questions.

Reflection is how we see things from our past as we are healing and how we can move forward and be in the now. In today's lesson you will be writing again in your journal, only a paragraph or two, on what you've noticed so far in the course. This exercise will cause you to think back so that you can see how your feelings come out on paper. Once you finish, keep it in a safe place because we will be using it in the days to come. Also make an appointment this week to talk about what you have experienced these past few days.

Affirmation for the Day

"I AM NOW CONNECTING WITH THE UNIVERSE AND BECOME ONE WITH ALL KNOWLEDGE."

✓ Say this three times in succession morning and evening.

Manifestation Course Day 4~ A New Awakening

Today is a new awakening for you. Let's begin with gratitude:

"Give thanks, today and every day, for all of your blessings. Remember to always bless your day and to be in a state of gratitude. Being in a state of gratitude for what is already in your life will help you to attract that which is what you want. Once you are in this state of being things will automatically begin to manifest for you.
If you have any negative thoughts or feelings take a moment to bless them with love and light. Ask your Angels to bring peaceful thoughts to you as you release the burden of these thoughts to them."

"Love yours Self and know that your awakening process will bring on many positive effects and as such, there will be times that you will be tested. You were chosen not because you are weak but because you have a great strength from within. You will be growing spiritually from this day on."

"Now close your eyes and feel the changes made in these last three days. Pay close attention to the days that follow as you will be seeing many new changes. Write it all down to record the progress you are making."

Affirmation for the Day

"I am growing stronger and wiser each day."

"I am an abundant being of light and I dare to prosper now."

"Love is everywhere and love is all I receive."

Say this three times in succession in the morning and night.

Manifestation Course Day 5

"You are now on your way to a new, true spiritual journey that will fill you and others with happiness. At some point the ego will start to fight. Allow the ego-thoughts to come in and as they do recognize what they are and then send them to the Angels. Ask the Angels to help you release the ego and you will be amazed at the new experience. Trust your Self."

"The new you is starting to connect with the Universal Truth. Allow the peace and joy of being connected to resonate with you."

Today write two paragraphs in your journal regarding your past five days. Re-experience these lessons that have been given to you. Allow your Self to be creative and let what comes to your mind flow onto the pages in front of you. Whatever you are feeling, write it down. When you are finished, email it to me and I will explain the changes that you are going through.

√ **Affirmation for the Day**

"I am now letting go and releasing my ego to the universe."

"I am now receiving Divine energy."

"Love is my truth and I dare to rejoice in it now."

Repeat these words in the morning and evening three times in succession.

1.2.18

√ **Manifestation Course Day 6**

"You should be seeing great results from the course if you have followed it correctly and without deviation from the process. Your energy level should start to improve and you will be led to start taking better care of your body.
Your body is the physical being that holds home to your spiritual Self and another part of this journey is to clear all energies that will help you to align with the Universe. When we clear and take care of our physical being you will begin to see more manifestations come to you because your body is the home of your spirit."

Today I want you to make a list of what you eat. Start by removing one item of processed food daily. This includes items that are made with white flour, white sugar, and/or over indulgence in alcohol. This may seem difficult to follow at first but processed foods affect the natural rhythms of your body flow and impede your ability to focus on meditating on manifestations. Meats are great sources of protein, which is very necessary for your body, but we must stay clear of meats that are not organic, free range or kosher. If that is not possible stick to free range or organic chicken and fish.

Water is a must. You need to start drinking more water and cut soft drinks from your diet as these beverages are high in sugar, sodium and additives. It is senseless to intake liquids that pose no nutritional value to you. It is also important to move your body freely through any type of exercise so as to allow the energy (chi or prana) flow through your body with more ease.

You will start to hear your Angels more when the body is removed of toxins. Give your body two weeks to adjust, don't give up and maintain your food journaling for the duration of this course. You will see beautiful results in your energy levels and your body and you will have a strong sense of knowing come over you.

Affirmation for the Day

"I am grateful for a new me."
"I now receive all blessings of Oneness and nothing can stop me now."

Say this three times in succession in the morning and evening and watch the results!

✓ **<u>Manifestation Course Day 7</u>**

You should be feeling positive energy and many changes. Today will be a simple day of lessons. I want you to re-examine the past seven days and write a summary of what changes have come. Once that is done, I want you to e-mail your summary to me and I will go over it, explaining what improvements need to be made and/or how well you are doing.

There is a lot of meaning behind the writing. Please email me within the next two days.

<u>Affirmation for the day</u>

"All is manifesting in my life now."

"I am blessed with all that is good for me and my family."

"I reach and everything manifests in my life."

Say this three times in succession morning and evening.

✓ Manifestation Course Day 8

You are now starting to see results. Trust your feelings because you are starting to connect with your higher Self. The Angels are now communicating through your thoughts at this point and if you get a hunch to do something then I suggest taking action as this is your intuitive sense coming to life.

You should take action at the time you have a great feeling to do so because it is powered by the Angels, the Universe and all the loving energy flowing through you now.

Today, we are going to ask the Angels to manifest something for us within the next week. Write down seven things you want to see manifested. Ask the Angels to put you in contact with the people and places to make it happen. Ask that they bring it fast with no harm coming to others. Use the words *"In seven days I am now manifesting…"*

Example: "I am now manifesting a chocolate swirl ice cream cone."

Manifest now.

Don't forget to be realistic in your goals. You do not want to say "In seven days I am now manifesting to be the richest man in the world."

Write down your Seven Day Manifestation and keep it in your journal. Open it on day eight and see how much has manifested.

Suggestion: Go forward 8 days in your journal and write a note to yourself reminding you to go over your Seven Day Manifestation Exercise. This will help you not to forget and go off the flow of your lessons.

Affirmation for the day

"I am successful in all my endeavors and I dare to manifest now."

Say three times in succession morning and evening.

Manifestation Course Day 9

Today is a day to show the teacher what you can now do. Within two days, write a paragraph or two of what you see for yourself in the next 6 months. Concentrate and let the energy flow. This is something you need to do to show how connected you are with your Angels and the higher Source. You will use your intuition and clairvoyance.

Follow these simple steps:

Close your eyes, be in silence, and ask your Angels to connect with your guides.
Say *"I now want to see what is in store for me in the next six months."* Get a paper and pen and start writing what comes to you. Once you are done, send it to me via email. I will respond once I've had a chance to review.

Whatever comes out, write it down. Don't try to analyze it. Trust your angels and know that whatever is coming out is the truth, even if it is several pages long. This will show me how in tune you have become with the universe since you've started the course.

Affirmation for the Day

"I am now in my complete power and I dare to connect fully to the Universe now."

Say three times in succession, in the morning and night.

Manifestation Course Day 10

Let's take some steps for your financial success. First if you have online banking you can use this step. Close your eyes before entering your pin to check your balance. Say three times, *"I have more than plenty."*

Next, visualize your balance going up. See the numbers rising. Never use the word DEBT for anything. Say, *Payoff all high balances."* Try this for the next two weeks and you will be amazed what happens when your energy is aligned and in the right place.

Keep up the positive work!

Affirmation for the Day

"I reach and all that is good comes to me."

Manifestation Course Day 11

Today is a wonderful day for you. You are starting to consciously feel the change and knowing that comes with it. In addition, there are many other changes, some you will question and others you will **KNOW**. That is part of the change in the level of vibration. If you are not feeling a connection at this point, go back. In addition, go within and ask yourself what part of the ego and fear are being held within you.

You may need to go back to the first lesson on *Release* if are not feeling changes.

When you are feeling connected and are not doubting, but moving forward, you will begin to see more manifestations in your life. These manifestations will continue as you grow more conscious and powerful. Remember what you see in the physical world is not your reality anymore. You are now the creator of your reality.

Once again, ask your Angels to manifest something for you. Something simple, like a short wait in the doctor's office or a parking place in front of your favorite store.

You are the creator of your life and your vibration is the key to manifesting all.

Affirmation for the Day

"I am truly blessed with the gifts that are manifesting in my life."

Say this three times in succession in the morning and evening.

Manifestation Course Day 12

Changes are being made in your life and there is more to come. This lesson is on *Love* and helping you to manifest your **Twin Flame**. If you already have your twin flame, this will energize that connection and keep you on a positive track.

These tools are simple yet very effective:

Write a letter in your journal describing exactly what you want in a mate. Be very specific and describe hair color, eye color, personality traits and any other characteristics you deem important.

If you already have your life partner, simply make a list of the things you love about that person. Once you start, you will probably realize that there are many things you take for granted. Give thanks and you will begin to see more and more of these positive traits. There will be a sense of renewed love and energy in your relationship and that energy will flow throughout your family and household.

This exercise will work quickly as long as you stay positive and know that what it is you wish to manifest is coming *Now.*

Affirmation for the Day

"I am now manifesting my Twin Flame and I dare to manifest it now."

Say this three times in succession in the morning and evening.

Manifestation Course Day 13

You are getting stronger in your ability to manifest. Your manifestations might come in different ways but you will be manifesting something every day. Stay focused because you will be tested with fear and doubt. Remember to release the fear and doubt into the Universe. Ask your Angels to help you and you will feel a sense of calming peace.

Today I want you to do something fun for you. It doesn't have to be anything big or time consuming, just take the time to do something you love to do. Pamper yourself and feel loved. When you love your Self, the energy is so vibrant that it radiates from within. Others will be drawn to your positive light and that loving energy will then spill over into every aspect of your life.

You are coming into your power and you are feeling the change. Get out your journal and write about the changes you've felt so far. If you wish, send it to me via e-mail. I would love to see your results.

Affirmation for the Day

"I (fill in your name) am in full high vibration and I am manifesting it all now."
Say this three times in succession in the morning and evening.

Manifestation Course Day 14

Today we need to give *Thanks* and *Appreciation* to all the people around you.
Make a list of people whom you love and appreciate having in your life. Write them a hand written note, letting them know how much they mean to you and mail it. You may also choose e-mail. It could be people who have helped you in the past, a friend you haven't spoken to in years or your parents, spouse and children. Once they receive the note, it will be a bright spot in their day and the blessings will come back to you ten-fold.

Once that is done, write a letter in your journal to yourself. Give thanks to yourself for the things that you do for you.

Savor the wonderful feeling of doing something good for yourself and others.

Affirmation for the Day

"I am now blessed with all that is good and *I Thank You*."

Manifestation Course Day 15

Love is the *Energy* you will receive by reading this. You are now aligned with the energy of the Angels and Angels are all around you. At this point, you have made a lot of progress. Today is a day to relax and enjoy the beauty around you.

For ten minutes, relax and meditate. Ask your Angels to show you what is to come. Close your eyes and visualize the next few days. When you are in your meditation, visualize that the days to come are happening now. Let everything that comes to you in your head flow. When you are finished, write everything down in your journal. Write down what you saw and what is still coming to you.

Affirmation for the Day

"I am connected to the Universe and I dare to prosper now."

Say three times in succession in the morning and evening.

Manifestation Course Day 16

We are made out of love and light and we all express ourselves differently. Today I want you to express your love to others either in words or deeds. You can also express this love in your journal.

The next thing is *Joy*. I want you to write a four line poem expressing *Joy*. It doesn't have to rhyme, just write down what comes to you. This will help you resolve past hurtful emotions.

Today release and send love to all as I am sending it to you now.

Love is you
Love is all
Love is a miracle
Love is joy
Love is remembering all that makes us smile.

Affirmation for the Day

"Love is all and I am Love."

Manifestation Course Day 17

You are on your way to a complete and new life. *Allowing* is the lesson for today. Let the loving energy of giving and receiving fill your heart. You need to *Allow* in order to receive your blessings. This is one of the key ingredients to manifesting all.

When someone offers you a gift, accept it. Never turn it down because if you do, that stops the flow. When you *Allow* the energy of giving (that includes receiving) to flow, it grows and you receive the higher vibration and all the blessings that accompany it.

Start allowing the energy to flow and see the light from above come down and bless you as you are now open to receive all good things from the Universe. This loving energy keeps you protected, aligned and happy.

Affirmation for the Day

"I am now allowing the higher vibrations to come into my life and all is wonderful."

Say this three times in succession in the morning and evening.

Manifestation Course Day 18

If you haven't been doing it already, you need to start keeping a daily journal. You need to keep track of your daily activities and at the end of the day you will also write down your thoughts and feelings. There is a journal attached to this course but of course if you feel drawn to write your thoughts and experiences down on something else, please feel free to do so, after all this is about you.

Also, make daily notes of what you are manifesting into your life. *Visualize* and *Realize* as if it were happening now.

How are you doing with the cutback of processed foods? Now is a good time to remember to incorporate daily exercise into your routine. Take a walk around the block or do a quick exercise video. You will feel better mentally and physically and this will keep you aligned with the higher vibration.

Tonight, bless the day and look forward to tomorrow.

Affirmation for the Day

"I am Balanced and aligned with the highest Vibration Now!"

Manifestation Course Day 19

Make a list of everything that has brought you joy during these past six months. Underline the most joyous experience that you have had. E-mail me an outline of your most joyous day.

Give thanks for all the joyful days to come and allow your Self to feel the presence of Joy.

Affirmation for the Day

"I am now Joyous in everyday moments."

Say three times in succession in the morning and evening.

Manifestation Course Day 20

Manifesting is an art that takes time and commitment to attain. Let's begin by clearing your mind and visualize happy moments of the past. Add to those happy moments by visualizing happy moments that are coming to your future. As you visualize your desires into reality, feel the thought and see it manifesting. The key to this exercise is relaxation. You must relax and know that you are manifesting all now.

Release your visions to the higher vibration of the Angels. Ask them to help you manifest all that you desire. Stick to the feeling and the knowing that it is happening now. Always keep the energy positive and know that your dreams are already happening.

Some of these lessons may seem repetitive in actions to you but you must understand that we are now incorporating new habits to your daily life. These new habits require practice and repetition. Trust in the guidance of the Angels…they have nothing but the most loving intentions towards you and all of humanity.

Affirmation for the Day

"I am my creator of my life and I am now manifesting all."

Manifestation Course Day 21

ACTION

ALLOWING

KNOWING

These are the tools to mastering the Course.

ACTION- Take action in what you want to manifest. For example: If you want to get a job interview, send your resume to many companies and ask the Angels to help you to have that resume fall into the right hands, for the benefit of all involved. Take action and see results. We cannot wish to manifest and then sit back and do nothing. The Angels will inspire you to take action for a reason…to see your wishes become reality.

ALLOWING- Allow the energy and request to work to the highest vibration. Be patient and allow yourself to trust that the Angels are working for you.

KNOWING- The act of knowing will complete the manifestation. Remember, see it, feel it, and it will be. Faith and Trust is what the Universal Energy works on.

These are simple tools but are very powerful. You are on your way to success.

Please email me your testimonials and remember—*ACTION, ALLOW and KNOWING*.

Affirmation for the Day

"I am blessed and am now manifesting all."

Repeat three times in succession in the morning and evening.

Manifestation Course Day 22

Today's lesson is *Clarity*. Meditate for ten minutes and ask your Angels to give you Clarity on what is in store for you in the coming weeks. Have your journal handy to write down what comes to mind. Allow your feelings and creativity to flow on the pages. Once you have written down what you see, keep it in a safe place because you will need to review it again in a couple of days.

Once you review, you will see messages in the writing. The Angels are trying to show you your path.

Affirmation for the Day

"I am the Creator of my life and I dare to prosper now."

Say three times in succession in the morning and evening.

Manifestation Course Day 23

Today I want you to get out your journal and write a paragraph about the changes that have been made in your life as a result of this course. Once you've finished, look it over and see what changes you would still like to see in the coming week. Then, write a letter to your Angels and ask them to help you accomplish these goals. Read your letter aloud and say it with true loving energy. Know that they are already manifesting your goals into reality.

Take notes on what happens in the coming week. Remember you are the creator of your universe and there is no place for doubt or fear. Allow your blessings to come into your life and you will realize all of your dreams.

You are now coming into your true power.

Affirmation for the Day

"I am the creator of my Universe and I dare to prosper now."

Say this three times in succession in the morning and evening.

Manifestation Course Day 24

You are now connecting to a higher vibration and in position to receive all. Remember that simple tools can be the most powerful in manifesting. Usually the simplest answer is the best answer.

You are coming into balance and experiencing a higher level of consciousness. Do not doubt all that you have learned.

Today I want you to visualize and ask your Angels to manifest three specific items within the next week. See your results and write down your experiences.

I also want you to create your own affirmation and repeat it over and over, either out loud or in your head. Email me and let me know how this works for you. You must allow the energy to work for you. Have faith and know that it is already working.

Affirmation for the Day

"I now receive all of my Blessings in the Present time which is *Now*.

Manifestation Course Day 25

As we heal our own spirit, we are also healing the earth. The Angels have given me a personal message that I am passing on to you.
They said to me,

"In Order to Heal the Earth You Have To Heal the People."
"The Earth and People Are One."

This lesson is about **Healing Within**. As we heal ourselves, we are also healing mother earth. You are one with all living things. Spread this message and we will make a positive change.
You can make a difference. Set a goal today to take action. Inspire a coworker or friend to think positively and you love will be sent to all as you create a spontaneous chain of positive energy from your actions.

"Change one person and you will change the world."

Pick up a piece of trash in the street and inspire one other person to do the same. Donate time or money to a worthy cause. Inspire someone else to do the same.

Making the earth a better place is not only a positive change for us but for generations to come.

Affirmation for the Day

"I am making a difference and am *Now* healing the world as I speak these words."

Say this three times in succession in the morning and evening.

"I am Inspired always by the creator divine source"

Manifestation Course Day 26

Today is a day to explore. What actions have you been taking with the guidance of this course? What are you allowing into your life now? What have you learned about knowing? How are you helping yourself and others?

Now is the time to go back into your journal and review all that you have experienced. Put the process together and send me a one page summary of your experiences.

Allow you to be one with the Universe and start manifesting all now. Put these principles to the test!

Affirmation for the Day

"I am one with the Universe and I dare to Prosper now."

Say three times in succession in the morning and evening.

Manifestation Course Day 27

This next exercise is a meditation. You may want to record this meditation with your own voice and then play it back and let yourself be guided in this process.

"Close your eyes now and visualize going to a place that you call paradise. It can be an island, mountains or forest. Wherever you feel the most relaxed. Visualize a white light around you. Now add a purple ray. See it wrapping around you and the bubble of white light. Once you have visualized all of this, call upon your Angels. Ask them to manifest something you desire."

Once you feel like you've made the connection, take yourself back to physical reality. Wait a week and watch the results as they manifest.

Affirmation for the Day

"I am one with Love and it is what I accept in my life now."

"Love is Miracle and I dare to have love now."

"I am protected and now manifest all in my life now."

Say this three times in succession in the morning and evening

Manifesting Course Day 28

This is your second meditation exercise that will help you to connect to your Angels.. Again, record this meditation in your own voice, speaking softly and slowly and allow yourself to be guided in this process. Remember to have some smooth relaxing music to calm you and keep you peaceful.

First, I want you to relax and get comfortable and in a quiet place and you must be
Relaxed and ready to take yourself to the Higher Vibration and go into a place in which you will contact your Angels.

"Close your eyes and take yourself to a place of paradise of your choice. For example, I take myself to an ocean setting where I meet up with my Angels and Guides.
Once you visualize yourself there bring in the White Light of protection, which comes from the Universal Source and envision yourself in a white bubble. Once you are in the bubble, add the purple ray of light which you wrap it around the bubble you have formed.
Now that you are protected and in the higher vibration, ask for your Angels and Guides to appear in your space and watch them appear to you, once they have appeared to you ask them to identify themselves to you.

This is an opportunity to ask your angels to help you on all that you want to manifest and believe me they will talk to you back through thoughts or you will hear them in your meditation. When they are in your presence ask them to align you and keep you in the higher vibration always. Once you have asked them to do so and asked them to manifest your request, thank your Angels and Guides and bring yourself back to awareness to the now. Open your eyes and feel the difference and you will feel a peace and a knowing.
Keep a journal and write down anything that the Angels said to you during your meditation."

In a week, you will see the manifestation come to fruition.

Blessings,
Written by
Anna M Simon

This is the last day of this Powerful Miracle Course

You have completed a course where there is No Passing or Failing Grade. This course is wonderful in that you will always have it and may go back to it at any point in your life, you are the co-creator of your destiny and when you begin to realize that you do indeed have the gift to manifest all in your life you will have mastered this course.

True Angel Guidance Community is all of us becoming one with the One and sending the right message to Heal the world by enlightening all and staying within the higher vibration of the Divine Energy, which is God Consciousness and is the All.

You have a set of beginning powerful tools to help you to be successful in your life. Share your knowledge for good and to help the people around your life open up their awareness. At this point you should be manifesting all in your life and if you need to read it again, do so. It is in your subconscious and you will remember immediately when you ask. When you ask, know that it will be indeed given. If you follow the heart of the course; *Action, Allowing and knowing* you will continue to manifest all.

I want to thank you for giving me this opportunity to teach you the tools for manifesting all with my Powerful Miracle Manifestation Course.
I will like to hear from you, just email Anna at www.Trueangelguidance.com. Let us make this world a better place by spreading that which you have learned. Awaken all and enlighten them so they too can spread the word to all. You are on your way to manifesting all now!

I am sending Love and Energy to you all. "May you always be protected in the Higher Vibration?"

"To Heal the World You Must Heal the People"

"Let's make a difference"

"Love is a Miracle and let's spread more love"
Blessings to you always, may you keep this information close to your heart.

The World's Best Metaphysical Teachers

- Top 10 best metaphysical teachers in the world:
- In 6th Place:
- Doreen Virtue (USA)
- In 7th Place:
- Dolores Cannon (USA)
- In 8th Place:
- Lisa Williams (USA)
- In 9th Place:
- Reverend Diane Davis (USA)
- In 10th Place:
- Dennis Binks (UK/Angleterre)

- Top 15 best metaphysical teachers in the world:
- In 11th Place:
- Anna Robles Simon (USA)

Anna Robles Simon (USA).

<u>Manifestation Course: Journal</u>

_____

_____

_____

_____

_____

_____

_____

_____

_____

_____

_____

_____

_____

_____

_____

_____

_____

_____

_____

_____

_____

_____

_____

_____

_____

_____

_____

_____

_____

_____

_____

_____

_____

_____

_____

_____

_____

_____

_____

_____

_____

_____

_____

_____

_____

_____

_____

_____

_____

_____

_____

_____

_____

_____

_____

_____

_____

_____

_____

_____

_____

_____

_____

_____

_____

_____

_____

_____

_____

_____

_____

_____

_____

_____

_____

_____

_____

_____

_____

_____

_____

_____

_____

_____

_____

_____

_____

_____

_____

_____

_____

_____

_____

_____

_____

_____

_____

_____

_____

_____

_____

_____

_____

_____

_____

_____

_____
_____
_____
_____
_____
_____
_____
_____
_____
_____
_____
_____
_____

_____
_____
_____
_____
_____
_____
_____
_____
_____
_____
_____
_____
_____
_____
_____
_____
_____
_____
_____
_____

_____

_____

_____

_____

_____

_____

_____

_____

_____

_____

_____

_____

_____

_____

_____

_____

_____

_____

_____

_____

_____

_____

_____

_____

_____

_____

_____

_____

_____

_____

_____

_____

_____

_____

_____

_____

_____

_____

_____

_____

_____

_____

_____

_____

_____

_____

_____

_____

_____

_____

_____

_____

_____

_____

_____

_____

_____

_____

_____

_____

_____

_____

_____

_____

_____

_____

_____

_____

_____

_____

_____

_____

_____

_____

_____

_____

_____

_____

_____

_____

_____

_____

_____

_____

_____

_____

_____

_____

_____

_____

_____

_____

_____

_____

_____

_____

_____

_____

_____

_____

_____

_____

_____

_____

_____

_____

_____

_____

_____

_____

_____

_____

_____

_____

_____

_____

_____

_____

_____

_____

_____

_____

_____

_____

_____

_____

_____

_____

_____

_____

_____

_____

_____

_____

_____

_____

_____

_____

_____

_____

_____

_____

_____

_____

_____

_____

_____

_____

_____

_____

_____

_____

_____

_____

_____

_____

_____

_____

_____

_____

_____

_____

_____

_____

_____

_____

_____

_____

_____

_____

_____

_____

_____

_____

_____

_____

_____

_____

_____

_____

_____

_____

_____

_____

_____

_____

_____

_____

_____

_____

_____

_____

_____

_____

_____

_____

_____

_____

_____

_____

_____

_____

_____

_____

_____

_____

_____

_____

_____

_____

_____

_____

_____

_____

_____

_____

_____

_____

_____

_____

_____

_____

_____

_____

_____

_____

_____

_____

_____

_____

_____

_____

_____

_____

_____

_____

_____

_____

_____

_____

_____

_____

_____

_____

_____

_____

_____

_____

_____

_____

_____

_____

_____

_____

_____

_____

_____

_____

_____

_____

_____

_____

_____

_____

_____

_____

_____

_____

_____

_____

_____

_____

_____

_____

_____

___

_____

_____

_____

_____

_____

_____

_____

_____

_____

_____

_____

_____

_____

_____

_____

_____

_____

_____

_____

_____

_____

_____

_____

_____

_____

_____

_____

_____

_____

_____

_____

_____

_____

_____

_____

_____

_____

_____

_____

_____

_____

_____

_____

_____

_____

_____

_____

_____

_____

_____

_____

_____

_____

_____

_____

_____

_____

_____

_____

_____

_____

_____

_____

_____

_____

_____

_____

_____

_____

_____

_____

_____

_____

_____

_____

_____

_____

_____

_____

_____

_____

_____

_____

_____

_____

_____

_____

_____

_____

_____

_____

_____

_____

_____

_____

_____

Powerful Miracle Manifestation Book, copyright
©2017 Anna M Simon

_____

_____

_____

_____

_____

_____

_____

_____

_____

_____

_____

_____

_____

_____

_____

_____

_____

_____

_____

_____

_____

_____

_____

_____

_____

_____

_____

_____

_____

_____

_____

_____

_____

_____

_____

_____

_____

_____

_____

_____

_____

_____

_____

_____

_____

_____

_____

_____

_____

_____

_____

_____

_____

_____

_____

_____

_____

_____

_____

_____

_____

_____

_____

_____

_____

_____

_____

_____

_____

_____

_____

_____

_____

_____

_____

_____

_____

_____

_____

_____

_____

_____

_____

_____

_____

_____

_____

_____

_____

_____

_____

_____

_____

_____

_____

_____

_____

_____

_____

_____

_____

_____

_____

_____

_____

_____

_____

_____

_____

_____

_____

_____

_____

_____

_____

_____

_____

_____

_____

_____

_____

_____

_____

_____

_____

_____

_____

_____

_____

_____

_____

_____

_____

_____

_____

_____

_____

_____

_____

_____

_____

_____

_____

_____

_____

_____

_____

_____

_____

_____

_____

_____

_____

_____

_____

_____

_____

_____

_____

_____

_____

_____

_____

_____

_____

_____

_____

_____

_____

_____

_____

_____

_____

_____

_____

_____

_____

_____

_____

_____

_____

_____

_____

_____

_____

_____

_____

_____

_____

_____

_____

_____

_____

_____

_____

_____

_____

_____

_____

_____

_____

_____

_____

_____

_____

_____

_____

_____

_____

_____

_____

_____

_____

_____

_____

_____

_____

_____

_____

_____

_____

_____

_____

"I am a child of a loving God and I dare to manifest now."

_____

_____

_____

_____

_____

_____

_____

_____

"Thank you and remember all is possible"

Inspired by the Creator

Written by Anna M Simon

Made in the USA
San Bernardino, CA
31 March 2017